ethnic cooking the microwave way

From the coast of Greece comes *pśari plakí,* a traditional main dish of tender fresh fish smothered in tomatoes and onions and seasoned with parsley, olive oil, and lemon. (Recipe is on page 35.)

ethnic cooking the MICROWAVE way

NANCY CAPPELLONI

PHOTOGRAPHS BY ROBERT L. AND DIANE WOLFE

easy menu
ethnic
cookbooks

Lerner Publications Company ▪ Minneapolis

Editor: Barbara L. King

Additional photographs and illustrations courtesy of Laura Westlund, pp. 6-7, 8, 11, borders; Jeanette Swofford, pp. 15, 17, 20. Photo on p. 12 reproduced with permission of the copyright owner, General Electric Company.

This book is available in two bindings:
Library binding by Lerner Publications Company
Soft cover by First Avenue Editions
241 First Avenue North
Minneapolis, Minnesota 55401

Special thanks to my international friends who generously shared their recipes with me, and to Bob, Lauren, Lisa, and Dora for their continued encouragement, enthusiasm, and love

Library of Congress Cataloging-in-Publication Data

Cappelloni, Nancy.
  Ethnic cooking the microwave way / Nancy Cappelloni ; photographs by Robert L. and Diane Wolfe.
     p.   cm. — (Easy menu ethnic cookbooks)
  Includes index.
  ISBN 0-8225-0929-6 (lib. bdg.)
  ISBN 0-8225-9660-1 (pbk.)
  1. Cookery, International—Juvenile literature.   2. Microwave cookery—Juvenile literature.   [1. Cookery, International.
2. Microwave cookery.]   I. Wolfe, Robert L., ill.   II. Wolfe, Diane, ill.   III. Title.   IV. Series.
TX725.A1C27   1994
641.5′882—dc20
                                          93-29543
                                             CIP
                                              AC

Manufactured in the United States of America

1 2 3 4 5 6 – I/JR – 99 98 97 96 95 94

Mexican hot chocolate, flavored with cinnamon and almond, is an easy treat with your microwave oven. (Recipe is on page 20.)

CONTENTS

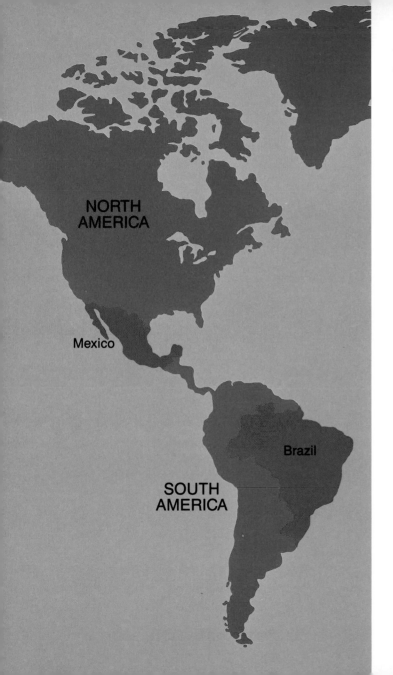

NORTH
AMERICA

Mexico

Brazil

SOUTH
AMERICA

INTRODUCTION

The microwave oven has become a common sight in North American kitchens. Yet many people use these ovens only to reheat leftovers or cook frozen dinners. They don't realize how easily and quickly delicious meals can be created in a microwave oven. By trying the wide variety of appealing international recipes in this book, you'll discover how useful your microwave oven is.

The recipes in this book come from 14 different countries around the world and represent diverse food traditions and cooking styles. Cooking the microwave way will save you time without losing authentic taste or appearance. A microwave oven allows you to add tasty ethnic foods, such as Italian *Risotto con Zucchine* and Israeli *Oaf Tapuzim,* to your daily menus with ease.

How a Microwave Oven Cooks

The power of microwaves (radio waves with the shortest wavelength) to heat food was discovered in 1946 by Percy Spencer while he was working with a radar system. As he stood in front of a working radar, a candy bar in his pocket melted. He spent several years experimenting with microwaves to harness their cooking ability. Spencer eventually patented the first microwave oven in 1952.

Inside a microwave oven, a device called a magnetron tube converts electricity into microwaves. These microwaves travel at the speed of light through your oven, the cooking dish, and the food inside it. As the microwaves pass through the food, they cause the food and water molecules to vibrate—at a rate of two and a half billion times per second! The vibrating molecules bump into each other, which creates friction. The heat produced by this friction cooks the food while leaving the air inside your oven cool.

Generally, microwaves penetrate and cook only the outer layers of food—the top, bottom, and sides. But a process called heat conduction, in which heat flows from the outside to the inside, carries heat to the center and cooks the food. Heat conduction eventually causes steam to build up and heat the cooking dish. Therefore, even though

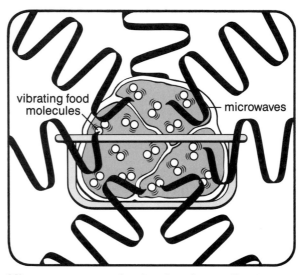

vibrating food molecules

microwaves

Microwaves cause food molecules to vibrate rapidly. The friction from these vibrations heats the food.

the air inside the oven stays cool, remember to use pot holders when removing dishes from your microwave oven. Heat conduction will also continue to cook the food even after the food is removed from the microwave oven. Many microwave recipes call for "standing time" after food is removed from the oven. Standing time allows this further heat conduction to take place.

All microwave ovens sold in the United States must follow certain government safety regulations. For instance, when you open a microwave oven door or the timer signals that the cooking time has ended, the magnetron and its microwaves automatically shut off. The magnetron cannot turn on as long as the oven door is open. As long as your microwave oven is in good condition, microwaves will not escape from your oven.

What's So Great about Microwave Cooking?

With a bit of practice, you'll find that cooking with your microwave oven has many advantages over traditional methods. Knowing what your oven can and cannot do will help you best use this modern technology.

Microwave ovens can defrost frozen foods and cook fresh ones much faster than stove burners and conventional ovens can. For the busy cook, this is an important advantage. In the traditional American style, a meal consists of several cooked dishes, all to be served at once. The microwave oven can cook or reheat one dish while other dishes are prepared on the burners or in the oven of the kitchen stove. To further reduce oven-to-table time, most recipes can be microwaved and served in the same container.

Nutritionists know that the less time food is exposed to heat, the better it will retain its nutritional value. A few minutes of microwaving, instead of hours of roasting or simmering, conserves vitamins and minerals as well as time.

Still, microwave ovens don't cook everything exactly as conventional ovens do. Food can be thoroughly cooked by microwaves but will not brown. The brown color and outer crust of meat and breads indicate to us that the food is completely cooked. Yet if you tried to cook these foods in a microwave oven long enough to brown them, you would instead overcook or burn them. Therefore, dishes that traditionally have a brown or toasted crust can be finished in a conventional oven or coated with a brown sauce for the desired appearance.

BEFORE YOU BEGIN

Whether you use traditional or microwave cooking methods, cooking any dish is easier and more fun if you are familiar with its ingredients. The international dishes in this book make use of some ingredients you may not know. You should also be familiar with the special cooking terms that will be used in these recipes. Therefore, before you start cooking any of the dishes in this book, study the following microwave instructions and cooking definitions very carefully. Then read through the recipe you want to try from beginning to end.

Now you are ready to shop for ingredients and to organize the cookware you will need. Once you have assembled everything, you can begin to cook. It is also very important to read *The Careful Cook* on page 44 before you start. These guidelines will make your microwave cooking experience safe, fun, and easy.

MICROWAVE TIPS

Microwave Cookware

Most manufacturers now label their glass, ceramic, paper, and some plastic cookware "microwave-safe," "microwave-proof," or "suitable for microwave." These dishes will not absorb microwaves but will allow the waves to pass through to cook the food. Microwavable glass cookware is suggested for the recipes in this book because glass heats well. Whatever cookware you use, be sure it is microwave-safe.

Containers made of metal or trimmed with metal are *not* safe for microwave cooking. Metal does not allow the micro-waves to pass through it. Instead, microwaves bounce off metal, which can cause bluish sparks or "arcs" inside your oven. These arcs can damage the oven and start a fire. Recycled paper products are not safe for microwave cooking because they often contain specks of metal.

Your cooking dish should be large enough to allow you to stir the food during prepara-tion and to prevent it from boiling or spilling over. When you will be heating a liquid to the boiling point, you should use a dish with twice the capacity you really need. The recipes in this book specify the container size that is best for each dish.

In order to avoid dangerous spills while carrying hot food and liquid from oven to counter, you should use containers with a lip or handle that will give you a firm hold with a pot holder.

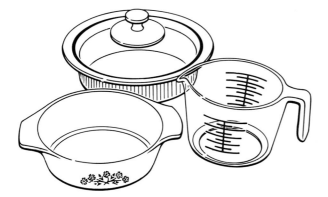

Be sure to select cookware that is microwave-safe and easy to handle.

Preparing and Arranging Food

Food that is already at room temperature will cook faster than chilled or frozen food. Ingredients for the recipes in this book are to be used at their normal storage temperatures. Cooking times and power levels have been adjusted to include refrigerated foods.

When chopping and preparing your ingredients, remember that food cooks faster and more evenly in a microwave oven when the pieces of food are all the same size. Thin, small pieces will cook faster than thick, large pieces.

For the food to cook evenly and quickly, it must be arranged properly in the microwave dish. Since microwaves do not fully penetrate food, the food along the outside of the dish cooks faster than the food on the inside. Place thinner or smaller pieces of food toward the center of the dish. Larger and thicker pieces should be placed around the outer edges.

Some foods cook faster than others. Vegetables cook faster than meat; porous vegetables, such as mushrooms, cook faster than dense vegetables, such as potatoes.

Arrange dense, heavy food around the outer edges of your dish. Place lighter, more porous foods in the center. Apples, potatoes, and other foods with non-porous skins must be peeled or pierced to prevent bursting in the microwave oven. Keep in mind that the more food you cook at one time, the longer it will take to heat through.

Covering Food

Covering food reduces cooking time by ensuring that moisture and heat stay inside the cooking dish. Covering helps to tenderize food, to prevent spattering and boiling over, and to cook food evenly.

Four types of covers work well in a microwave oven: glass casserole lids, microwave-safe plastic wrap, waxed paper, and microwave-safe paper towels. A glass lid or plate is often the best covering because it holds heat and moisture inside the dish and is easy to put on and take off. Plastic wrap also provides a tight cover that will keep in moisture and heat. In fact, after covering a dish snugly with plastic wrap, you should fold back a corner of the plastic wrap lid or cut a slit in the top to allow a little bit of steam to escape. Without this vent, the plastic wrap might split or sink into the food. Since steam builds up inside a covered container, always remove a cover by starting at the far edge and tilting the lid or wrap up and away from you. This will keep the escaping steam from burning you.

Microwave-safe plastic wrap is the perfect covering for many microwaved dishes.

Oven Wattage, Cooking Times, and Power Settings

Microwave ovens set to cook on high power do not all use the same amount of power. The lowest times indicated for cooking the recipes in this book are cooking times for a 600- to 700-watt oven. Some microwave ovens use only 400 to 600 watts of electrical power. To take into account the differences among microwave ovens, recipes usually give a range of cooking times. You may need to do some experimenting with your oven to determine its own cooking speed and power. Check the wattage of your oven in the manufacturer's operating manual. If your oven uses less power, you'll need to adjust the cooking time. For a 400- to 600-watt oven, add approximately 15 seconds of cooking time to each minute given in a recipe.

Microwave recipes often call for the use of different cooking levels. In this book, recipes specify either high power (HIGH), which is the normal setting of 100% of an oven's power, or medium power (MEDIUM), which is 60% to 70% of an oven's power. Check the operating manual for your oven to find out how to adjust your oven's cooking level.

Turning, Elevating, and Stirring Food

Food may cook unevenly in your microwave oven, but you can use several techniques to solve this problem. Between cooking cycles, try turning the dish clockwise a quarter turn to be sure the microwaves hit all outer surfaces of the food. Some microwave ovens come equipped with a carousel or turntable that turns automatically during the cooking cycle.

By elevating or raising the food you are cooking, you give the microwaves a chance to heat from the bottom of the dish. Elevate the food in your oven by placing the container on a microwave-safe trivet or a plate turned upside-down.

Stirring, turning, or rearranging food in the dish between cooking cycles will also help the food cook evenly and quickly. Since the outer surfaces of food cook faster than the inside, stirring redistributes the heat when the food is moved around. Turn over and rearrange large pieces of food to ensure even cooking throughout.

Standing Time

Most foods continue to cook for a few minutes after they are removed from a microwave oven. "Standing time," or the length of time a dish rests covered before it is served, is included in many recipes to allow the food to finish cooking completely.

"Hot Spots"

Foods with concentrated areas of fat, water, or sugar will develop "hot spots," or areas where the food is much hotter than the rest. When recipes call for ingredients that cook at different rates, you will notice that the ingredients that cook faster are added toward the end of preparation. Stirring the food and allowing some standing time will help to disperse the heat throughout the dish.

Checking for Doneness

To prevent overcooking, always cook food for the minimum amount of time given in the recipe. When the cooking time is up, allow the food to stand before checking to see if it looks done. If the food does not appear to be fully cooked, replace the dish in your oven and cook 30 to 60 seconds longer.

Once again, let the dish stand before checking for doneness.

Remember—ALWAYS UNDERCOOK! You can easily add cooking time, but if the food is overcooked, it's too late to fix it.

COOKING UTENSILS

kitchen mallet – A hammer-shaped tool with a large head specifically designed to pound meat to the desired thinness and tenderness

molinillo – A wooden beater with rings of different sizes on it, available in shops that specialize in Mexican goods

reamer – A bowl with a ridged, pointed dome in its center designed to extract juice from citrus fruit. Smaller handheld reamers are specially made to use with lemons and limes.

sieve – A metal basket of fine mesh used to drain food

slotted spoon – A spoon with small openings in its bowl used to pick solid food out of a liquid

whisk – A small wire utensil used for beating food by hand

COOKING TERMS

al dente – An Italian term, meaning literally "to the tooth." It means the point at which pasta or rice is properly cooked—firm and tender, but not soft.

baste – To pour, brush, or spoon liquid over food as it cooks, in order to flavor and moisten the food

boil – To heat liquid until bubbles form and rise rapidly to the surface

core – To remove the center part of a fruit or vegetable

dice – To chop food into small pieces

fillet – To remove bones from meat or fish

garnish – To decorate with small pieces of food

grate – To cut food into tiny pieces by rubbing it against a grater

marinate – To soak food in a liquid in order to add flavor and to tenderize it

mince – To chop food into very tiny pieces

pinch – A very small amount, usually what you can pick up between your thumb and forefinger

seed – To remove seeds from a fruit or vegetable

simmer – To cook over low heat in liquid kept just below the boiling point. Bubbles may occasionally rise to the surface.

SPECIAL INGREDIENTS

almond extract – A liquid made from the oil of the almond nut

arborio rice – A small-grain white rice from Italy that is used specifically for *risotto*

bay leaf – The dried leaf of the bay (also called laurel) tree used to season meats, poultry, or stews. It is always removed from the dish before serving.

cayenne—The finely ground dried pods and seeds of a variety of hot red chili peppers

Chinese cabbage—A pale green vegetable with broad, tightly packed leaves, sometimes referred to as *Napa* or *celery cabbage*

coriander—An herb made from coriander seeds, either whole or ground, that is used in many East Indian dishes

cornstarch—A fine, white powder made from corn, commonly used to thicken sauces and gravies

crushed red pepper flakes—Dried pieces of hot red peppers used to give a spicy flavor to foods

cumin—The seeds of an herb in the parsley family, used whole or ground to give food a pungent flavor

curry powder—A blend of six or more spices, including cumin, coriander, fennel, clove, cinnamon, and mustard seeds, that gives food a spicy flavor and a yellow color

dashinomoto—An instant powdered soup base from Japan that is made from *dashi,* the dried seaweed and *bonita* fish flakes that are essential ingredients of Japanese

cooking. *Dashinomoto* is available in stores that sell Japanese foods.

five-spice powder—A blend of ground star anise, fennel, cinnamon, cloves, and Szechwan (Chinese) peppercorns with a distinct, pungent flavor

garlic—An herb whose distinctive flavor is used in many dishes. Each bulb can be broken up into several sections called cloves. Remove the brittle, papery covering around each clove before chopping it up.

gingerroot—A knobby, light brown root used for flavor in Asian dishes. *Ground ginger* is made from the dried undergound stem of the ginger plant and tastes very different from fresh gingerroot.

glutinous rice – Also called *sweet* or *sticky rice,* a short-grain white rice that becomes very sticky when cooked

ground anise – The seed of a plant in the carrot family that is used ground to add a licorice flavor to food

ground fennel – The powdered seed of an herb in the carrot family

Gruyère cheese – A hard, light yellow cheese from Switzerland with a tangy flavor. Swiss cheese can be substituted in most recipes calling for Gruyère.

mung bean sprouts – Young shoots from the mung bean, eaten raw or mixed with other ingredients in stir-fried dishes

olive oil – An oil made from pressed olives that is used in salads and cooked dishes

paprika – A red powder made from the ground, dried pods of the capsicum pepper plant, used for its flavor and color

Parmesan cheese – A hard, sharply flavored Italian cheese usually grated for use in cooking

raclette cheese – A hard, strong-smelling cheese from Switzerland with a mild flavor

sesame seeds – Seeds from an herb grown in tropical climates. *Sesame oil,* strong in flavor, is pressed from sesame seeds.

shiitake mushrooms – Black mushrooms, available either dried or fresh, used in many Japanese recipes. The dried mushrooms must be soaked in warm water to make them tender before cooking.

soy sauce – A dark brown sauce made from soybeans and other ingredients. It is used instead of salt in Asian dishes.

split red lentils – Mild-flavored, bright orange dried beans sold in stores carrying Indian, Middle Eastern, or health foods

thyme – A fragrant herb from the leaves of a bushy shrub that grows mainly in California and France, used fresh or dried

turmeric – A yellow, aromatic spice made from the root of the turmeric plant

water chestnuts – Sweet, crisp root vegetables widely used in Chinese dishes

AN INTERNATIONAL MENU

Below is a simple menu for a varied, truly international meal that can be prepared with a microwave oven. The ethnic names of the dishes are given, along with a guide on how to pronounce them. At least one alternative for each stage of the meal is included.

ENGLISH NAME	ETHNIC NAME/ PRONUNCIATION GUIDE	COUNTRY
Beverages		
Hot Chocolate	Chocolate Mexicano (choh-koh-LAH-teh meh-hee-KAH-noh)	Mexico
Limeade	Nam Manao (nahm mah-NOW)	Thailand
Mint Tea	Thé (tay)	Morocco
Appetizers		
Marinated Mushrooms	Manitaria Marinata (mah-nee-TAH-ree-ah MAH-ree-NAH-tah)	Greece
Pearl Meatballs	Chêng-Nomi-Yüantzŭ (CHUNG-noh-ah-MEE-yoo-ENZ)	China
Soups		
Beaten Egg Soup	Kakitama-jiru (kah-kee-TAH-mah jee-roo)	Japan
Onion Soup with Cheese	Soupe à l'Oignon Gratinée (soop ah lwon-YOHN grah-tee-NAY)	France

ENGLISH NAME	ETHNIC NAME/ PRONUNCIATION GUIDE	COUNTRY
Side Dishes		
Rice with Zucchini	Risotto con Zucchine (ree-ZOH-toh cohn zoo-KEE-nay)	Italy
Bean Sprout Salad	Sukju Namul (sook-joo NAH-mool)	Korea
Red Lentil Curry	Masoor Dahl (muh-SOOR dahl)	Sri Lanka
Main Dishes		
Five Spice Beef	Wu Xiang Niu (woo shee-ohng noo)	China
Chicken with Oranges	Oaf Tapuzim (ohf tah-poo-ZEEM)	Israel
Baked Fish	Pśari Plakí (PSAH-ree plah-KEE)	Greece
Raclette	Raclette (rah-KLEHT)	Switzerland
Desserts		
Sweet Cooked Apples	Elma Tatlisi (EHL-mah taht-LEE-see)	Turkey
Baked Bananas	Banana Bacana (bah-NAH-nah BAH-cah-nah)	Brazil
Lemon Ice	Granita di Limone (grah-NEE-tah dee lee-MOH-nay)	Italy
Chocolate Fondue	Fondue Chocolat (fohn-DEW shoh-coh-LAH)	Switzerland

BEVERAGES

Most countries have a favorite beverage that is enjoyed with meals or as an afternoon refreshment. Drinks of chocolate, fruit juice, and tea are very popular throughout the world.

Hot Chocolate/
Chocolate Mexicano
Mexico

Tablets of Mexican chocolate, specially flavored with cinnamon, almonds, and sugar, can be purchased in Mexican or Latin American grocery stores. You can also blend your own "Mexican chocolate" with the same ingredients.

1 3-ounce cake of Mexican chocolate (or 3 ounces semisweet baker's chocolate or chocolate morsels, 1 teaspoon cinnamon, 2 tablespoons sugar, and ½ teaspoon almond extract)
4 cups milk

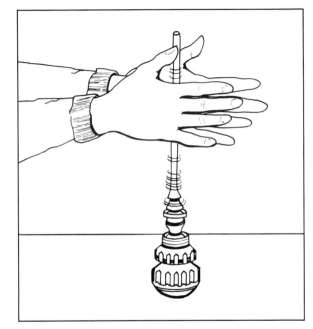

To use a *molinillo*, twirl the handle quickly between your palms. The twisting motion of the bottom rings will turn hot chocolate into a frothy drink.

1. Break chocolate into smaller pieces and place in a 2-quart microwavable glass measuring cup or handled bowl. (If you are using baker's chocolate or chocolate morsels, add cinnamon, sugar, and almond extract.) Stir in milk.

2. Microwave, uncovered, on HIGH for 4 minutes. Stir. Microwave on HIGH for 2 to 4 more minutes, or until the chocolate has melted and the milk is close to boiling. Very small bubbles will form on the surface and edges of the milk, which will begin to coat the container.

3. Whip with a wire whisk, egg beater, or *molinillo* until the chocolate has dissolved completely and the milk is frothy. (For extra-foamy hot chocolate, beat with an electric beater or pour in a blender and whip.)

4. Pour into mugs and serve hot.

Serves 4–5

Limeade/*Nam Manao*
Thailand

In very hot weather, this cold, refreshing drink is a welcome relief. Popular throughout Thailand, sweet and sour limeade is the perfect accompaniment to spicy Thai foods such as curry. (Lemons can be used instead of limes.)

7 to 9 fresh limes, cut in half
4 cups water
¾ cup sugar
pinch of salt
6 to 8 lime slices (for garnish)
fresh mint leaves

1. With your hands or a reamer, squeeze the juice from limes to make 1 cup of lime juice. Set juice and lime rinds aside.

2. Pour water into a 2-quart microwavable glass measuring cup or handled bowl. Microwave, uncovered, for 6 to 8 minutes on HIGH until almost boiling. Little bubbles will form on the water surface.

3. Add sugar and salt and stir until dissolved. Add lime rinds and let the mixture stand for 10 minutes until cool.

4. Squeeze the remaining juice from the rinds into the limeade and discard the rinds. Pour the limeade through a sieve into a pitcher. Add reserved lime juice and stir well. Refrigerate until ready to serve.

5. To serve, fill a tall glass with ice and add limeade. Garnish with a slice of lime and a sprig of mint, if desired.

Serves 6–8

Mint Tea/*Thé*
Morocco

Tea was introduced to Morocco in the 19th century by British traders returning from Asia and is now served throughout the day. Moroccan mint tea is very sweet.

4 cups water
4 teaspoons loose green tea
⅓ cup sugar
1 cup fresh mint leaves

1. Pour water into a 2-quart glass microwavable measuring cup or handled bowl. Cover and microwave on HIGH for 8 minutes or until just boiling. Little bubbles will appear on the water surface.
2. Add tea, sugar, and mint leaves. Cover with a heatproof glass lid or plate and let steep for 4 to 5 minutes. Stir gently.
3. Pour the tea through a sieve into glasses or teacups. Serve hot.

Serves 4–6

Add Mediterranean flavor to any meal with Moroccan mint tea or Greek marinated mushrooms.

APPETIZERS

Appetizers are enjoyed in many countries around the world, partly because they are so versatile. They can serve as a small meal, a course before a larger meal, or a nutritious snack.

Marinated Mushrooms/ *Manitaria Marinata* Greece

In Greece, people often stop at a taverna, or café, in the late afternoon to eat, socialize, and relax. They might enjoy olives, tomatoes, cheese, pastries, stuffed grape leaves, or marinated mushrooms. This dish combines flavors and ingredients that have made Greek cuisine famous— olive oil and herbs make a delicious dressing for fresh mushrooms.

**2 cloves garlic, peeled and thinly
    sliced
2 tablespoons fresh parsley, finely
    chopped
15 whole black peppercorns
½ teaspoon thyme
½ teaspoon oregano
 1 bay leaf
 1 pound fresh mushrooms, washed,
    stems trimmed
¼ teaspoon salt
⅓ cup olive oil
 2 tablespoons lemon juice**

1. In a round, shallow, microwavable casserole or pie plate, combine garlic, parsley, peppercorns, thyme, oregano, and bay leaf. Arrange mushrooms, stem sides down, in rings in the dish.
2. Microwave, uncovered, on HIGH for 4 to 5 minutes, or just until tender. Let cool for 10 minutes.
3. Drain excess cooking liquid. In a small bowl, whisk together salt, olive oil, and lemon juice. Pour this dressing over the mushrooms and mix to coat well.
4. Cover and refrigerate for at least 2 hours. Serve chilled.

Serves 8

Pearl Meatballs/ *Chêng-Nomi-Yüantzŭ* China

For over 1,000 years, Chinese dim sum (meaning "touch of heart" or "light of heart") has been a traditional midday meal made up of a selection of small appetizers, such as pearl meatballs. The rice coating on these meatballs resembles tiny pearls. In China, pearls are a symbol of good luck, wealth, and abundance. Popular in Shanghai and Beijing, pearl meatballs are traditionally steamed in a steamer.

1 cup uncooked glutinous rice (or short-grain white rice)
8 to 10 cups water
1 pound ground pork
¼ cup canned water chestnuts, drained and diced
1 egg, beaten well
1 large green onion, minced
2 tablespoons soy sauce
1 teaspoon peeled, minced fresh gingerroot
1 teaspoon cornstarch
6 whole Chinese cabbage leaves (or green cabbage)

1. Wash rice in a 1-quart microwavable glass measuring cup or bowl. Drain in a sieve. Return rice to the bowl, fill the bowl with water, and let the rice soak for 2 hours.
2. Drain the rice and refill with 2 cups of fresh water. Microwave, uncovered, on HIGH for 5 minutes. Let stand for 5 minutes. Drain well.
3. Spread the rice on a plate to dry for 10 to 15 minutes. The rice will be slightly sticky.
4. In a bowl, combine pork, water chestnuts, egg, green onion, soy sauce, gingerroot, and cornstarch. Blend thoroughly. With wet hands, form the mixture into small balls about 1 inch in diameter. Place the finished meatballs on a sheet of waxed paper.
5. Roll each meatball in rice, covering it completely. Continue until all meatballs are coated.

6. Measure 3 tablespoons of water into a microwavable 10- to 12-inch glass pie plate or round baking dish. Place 3 cabbage leaves in the bottom of the dish. Arrange 12 meatballs along the outer edge of the dish, leaving the center open and some space between the meatballs.
7. Cover with a microwavable lid or plate. Microwave on HIGH for 5 minutes. Carefully turn each meatball over. Move the ones nearest the center to the outer edge of the dish and the outer ones toward the center. Cover and microwave for 5 to 6 minutes on HIGH. Let stand, covered, for 5 minutes. Pierce a meatball with a fork to check that the meat is no longer pink.
8. Place the finished meatballs on a serving dish and cover with foil to keep warm. Repeat the microwaving process with remaining meatballs. Serve with soy sauce for dipping.

Makes 24 meatballs

Pearl meatballs (left), beaten egg soup (top, recipe on page 26), and bean sprout salad (right, recipe on page 30) bring the savory tastes of the Far East to your table.

SOUPS

Many cultures have a variety of traditional soups. Very simple soups may start a multi-course dinner, while thick and hearty soups make a meal by themselves.

Beaten Egg Soup/
Kakitama-jiru
Japan

The Japanese eat soup with every meal. A clear soup, like this one, usually begins a Japanese meal. Most Japanese soups are served in lacquered bowls with covers.

4 dried shiitake mushrooms (or 6 fresh mushrooms, washed, stems trimmed and discarded, caps thinly sliced)
2½ level teaspoons instant *dashino-moto,* dissolved in 4 cups water (or use 4 cups clear chicken broth in place of the *dashinomoto* and water)

1 egg, beaten well
1 green onion, finely sliced

1. If using dried mushrooms, soak them in a bowl of warm water for 15 to 30 minutes, as directed on the package. Drain. Trim the stems and discard. Thinly slice the caps.
2. Place dissolved *dashinomoto* (or chicken broth) in a 2-quart microwavable glass measuring cup or handled bowl. Microwave, uncovered, on HIGH for 4 minutes. Stir. Cover and microwave on HIGH for 7 to 9 minutes or until boiling. Use pot holders to remove the bowl from the oven, as it will be very hot.
3. Briskly stir in the beaten egg with a chopstick or fork to form threads of egg. (The soup must be boiling or the egg will not form threads.) Add mushroom slices.
4. Microwave, uncovered, on HIGH for 30 seconds. Ladle into individual bowls. Garnish each bowl with sliced green onions and serve.

Serves 4

Onion Soup with Cheese/
Soupe à l'Oignon Gratinée
France

In the traditional recipe, the onions in this soup are simmered in butter, oil, and soup stock for hours, until the soup develops a rich flavor and deep color. The classic Parisian onion soup makes a perfect lunch or light supper. Serve with a green salad, crusty French bread, cheese, and fruit.

2 to 3 large yellow onions, thinly sliced (about 4 cups)
1 tablespoon vegetable oil
3 tablespoons butter or margarine, cut into small pieces
½ teaspoon sugar
2 tablespoons white flour
3½ cups (28 ounces) canned beef broth
2 cups (16 ounces) canned chicken broth
6 slices French bread, ½-inch thick, well toasted
1½ cups grated Gruyère or Swiss cheese

1. In a 3-quart microwavable glass casserole or handled bowl, combine onions, oil, and butter or margarine. Cover tightly and microwave on HIGH for 4 minutes. Stir, cover, and microwave on HIGH for another 4 minutes.
2. Stir in sugar. Microwave, uncovered, on HIGH for 3 to 5 minutes or until the onions are tender. Stir in flour and microwave, uncovered, on HIGH for 1 minute.
3. Add beef and chicken broths and stir. Cover tightly and microwave on HIGH for 8 minutes. Stir, cover, and microwave on HIGH for another 10 to 12 minutes or until boiling. Use pot holders to remove. Stir. Cover and microwave on MEDIUM (60% power) for 4 minutes.
4. Ladle soup into 6 ovenproof soup bowls until they are almost full. Top each with a slice of toasted French bread and sprinkle with grated cheese. Place the bowls on a baking tray or cookie sheet under a preheated broiler for 2 to 3 minutes until the cheese is bubbly and lightly browned. Serve immediately.

Serves 6

Prepared in a microwave oven, creamy, cheesy Italian *risotto* is a foolproof side dish.

SIDE DISHES

A side dish has several traditional functions in a meal. In the United States, vegetables are usually served as an accompaniment to a main dish. In other countries, however, a side dish is served as a separate course or with two or three other side dishes at the same time.

Rice with Zucchini/ *Risotto con Zucchine* Italy

Traditional cooks in northern Italy always make risotto *over the stove, adding the liquid slowly and stirring constantly. In this microwave recipe, the* risotto *cooks quickly and keeps the proper* al dente *firmness.* Buon appetito!

2 tablespoons olive oil or vegetable oil
3 tablespoons butter or margarine, cut into 3 equal pieces

1 large clove garlic, minced
1 small yellow onion, finely chopped (about ⅔ cup)
1¾ cups (14 ounces) canned chicken broth
¼ cup water
2 medium zucchini, diced (about 2½ cups)
1 cup uncooked arborio rice (or short-grain white rice)
⅓ cup grated Parmesan cheese
1 tablespoon finely chopped fresh parsley
freshly ground black pepper

1. Combine oil, 1 tablespoon butter or margarine, garlic, and onion in a 3-quart microwave-safe casserole or handled bowl. Cover and microwave on HIGH for 3 minutes, or until onions are tender. Remove from oven and let stand, covered, while broth and zucchini are prepared.
2. Pour chicken broth and water in a 1-quart microwavable glass measuring cup. Microwave, covered, on HIGH for 2 minutes or until simmering. Let stand, covered, while zucchini is prepared.

3. Place zucchini and remaining butter or margarine in a 1-quart microwavable glass measuring cup or handled bowl. Cover and microwave on HIGH for 3 minutes or until bright green and almost tender. Let zucchini stand, covered, while rice is prepared.
4. Add rice to the onion and garlic mixture, stirring well to coat each grain. Add chicken broth. Cover tightly and microwave on HIGH for 4 to 6 minutes or until boiling. Then microwave on MEDIUM (60%) for 5 minutes.
5. Stir the zucchini and its cooking liquid into the rice. Cover and microwave on MEDIUM (60%) for 4 to 6 minutes, or until the rice has absorbed all liquid. The *risotto* should be *al dente*—tender but firm.
6. Stir in Parmesan cheese and parsley. Cover and let stand for 5 minutes. Add freshly ground pepper to taste and serve immediately.

Serves 6

Bean Sprout Salad/
Sukju Namul
Korea

Korean cuisine features a number of vegetarian dishes. Microwaving retains the color, crispness, and nutrients of vegetables, just as traditional stir-frying does.

¾ pound fresh mung bean sprouts, washed and drained
3 cloves garlic, minced
5 green onions, finely chopped
pinch of crushed red pepper flakes (optional)
5 teaspoons Korean or Japanese light soy sauce
2 teaspoons sesame oil
5 teaspoons Korean vinegar or apple cider vinegar
2 teaspoons toasted or untoasted sesame seeds

1. Place bean sprouts and garlic in a 2-quart microwavable glass casserole or handled bowl. Cover tightly and microwave on HIGH for 3 minutes, or until sprouts are tender but not soggy. Uncover and let cool for 5 minutes. Drain any cooking liquid. Add green onions and pepper flakes (if desired).
2. To make the dressing, mix soy sauce, sesame oil, vinegar, and sesame seeds in a small bowl. Pour over bean sprouts and lightly toss.
3. Allow the salad to stand at room temperature for ½ hour or longer. Stir again and serve. Leftovers can be refrigerated and served as a cold side dish.

Serves 4–6

Red Lentil Curry/
Masoor Dahl
Sri Lanka

2 tablespoons vegetable oil
1 small onion, finely chopped (about ¾ cup)
1 teaspoon ground coriander
½ teaspoon ground cumin
¼ teaspoon cayenne
¼ teaspoon ground fennel

⅛ teaspoon turmeric (or substitute
2⅛ teaspoons prepared curry
powder in place of all spices)
1 cup split red lentils, washed
2 cups water
salt
¼ to 1 teaspoon crushed red pepper
flakes (optional)

1. In a 2-quart microwavable glass casserole or handled bowl, combine oil and onion. Microwave, uncovered, on HIGH for 2 minutes or until tender.

2. Stir in coriander, cumin, cayenne, fennel, and turmeric (or prepared curry powder). Stir in the lentils to coat them with the spices. Add water and cover tightly. Microwave on HIGH for 6 to 8 minutes or just until boiling. Stir.

3. Cover tightly and microwave on MEDIUM (60%) for 3 to 6 minutes or until lentils are soft and most of the water has been absorbed.

4. Let the *dahl* stand, covered, for 15 minutes. Stir. Add salt and dried pepper flakes to taste, if desired.

Serves 4–6

Serve refreshing limeade from Thailand (recipe on page 21) with spicy red lentil curry from Sri Lanka.

Exotic ethnic main dishes, such as Chinese five spice beef (foreground) and Israeli chicken with oranges (left, recipe on page 34), are easily prepared in your microwave oven.

MAIN DISHES

Five Spice Beef/
Wu Xiang Niu
China

1 tablespoon vegetable oil
5 tablespoons soy sauce
1 tablespoon firmly packed brown
sugar
5 thin slices peeled gingerroot
1½ teaspoons cornstarch
1¼ teaspoons five-spice powder (or a
mixture of ¼ teaspoon each of
ground anise, fennel, clove,
cinnamon, and pepper)
1 tablespoon water or chicken broth
1 pound top sirloin or top round
steak, sliced into thin strips
¼ inch wide by 2 inches long
1 cup uncooked converted or long-
grain white rice
2 cups water
¼ teaspoon salt
1 green onion, thinly sliced
1 carrot, peeled and cut into thin strips

1. In an 8- by 8-inch microwavable glass baking dish, combine oil, soy sauce, brown sugar, gingerroot, cornstarch, five-spice powder (or the substitute spices), and water or chicken broth. Mix well. Arrange beef evenly in a single layer in the dish and refrigerate for at least 1 hour.
2. Combine rice, water, and salt in a 2-quart microwavable glass measuring cup or casserole. Stir, cover, and micro-wave on HIGH for 12 minutes. Let stand, covered, for at least 10 minutes.
3. Remove beef from the refrigerator and cover the dish tightly. Microwave on HIGH for 3 minutes. Stir to move uncooked portions to the outer edge of the dish and recoat the meat. Rearrange the meat in a single layer again. Cover and micro-wave on HIGH for 1 to 3 minutes, or until the meat is no longer red.
4. Serve the beef and its sauce with rice. Garnish with green onion and carrot.

Serves 4

Chicken with Oranges/ *Oaf Tapuzim*
Israel

In Israeli tradition, honey symbolizes the sweetness of the New Year or any happy occasion. Serve this chicken over rice, cooked barley, bulgur, or kasha.

¾ cup orange juice
¼ teaspoon ground ginger
¼ teaspoon paprika
4 teaspoons lemon juice
3 tablespoons honey
1 tablespoon freshly grated orange rind
2 tablespoons butter or margarine
4 skinless, boneless chicken breasts
    (1 to 1½ pounds)
1 level tablespoon cornstarch
    salt
1 orange, sliced (for garnish)
    sprigs of fresh parsley

1. In a 2-cup microwavable glass measuring cup, combine orange juice, ginger, ⅛ teaspoon paprika, lemon juice, honey, orange rind, and butter or margarine. Microwave, uncovered, on HIGH for 1½ minutes. Stir to combine.

2. With a kitchen mallet, pound chicken breasts between two sheets of waxed paper until they are ¼ inch to ½ inch thick.

3. In a shallow microwavable glass casserole or baking dish, arrange the chicken in a single layer, with thicker parts toward the outside of the dish. Pour all but ½ cup of the sauce over the chicken. Cover with waxed paper. Microwave on HIGH for 4 minutes.

4. Turn chicken pieces over and rearrange, placing less cooked parts toward the outside of the dish. Cover and microwave on HIGH for 4 to 6 minutes, or until the chicken is cooked. Let the dish stand, covered, for 5 minutes.

5. Meanwhile, add cornstarch to the remaining ½ cup of sauce and stir well with a wire whisk to remove any lumps.

6. With a slotted spoon, remove the chicken from the baking dish and place on a serving platter. Cover with aluminum foil to keep warm while sauce is prepared.

7. Add the cornstarch mixture to the sauce remaining in the baking dish. Cover and microwave on HIGH for 1½ minutes, or until the sauce has boiled and thickened. Stir well and pour the sauce over the chicken. Salt to taste. Garnish with orange slices, parsley, and remaining paprika.

Serves 4

Baked Fish/*Pśari Plakí*
Greece

With its traditional sauce of olive oil, lemon juice, and parsley, this recipe is also delicious when made with rock cod, salmon, sole, or sea bass.

1 medium onion, thinly sliced (¾ cup)
2 cloves garlic, minced
5 tablespoons olive oil
1½ pounds fresh red snapper fillets
    juice of 1 lemon (2 to 3 tablespoons)
5 tablespoons minced fresh parsley
1½ teaspoons thyme
2 large tomatoes, thinly sliced

1. In a 1-quart microwavable glass measuring cup, combine onion, garlic, and 2 tablespoons olive oil. Cover and microwave on HIGH for 3 to 4 minutes or until tender. Let stand, covered, until the fish is prepared.
2. Rinse fish fillets in cool water and pat dry with paper towels.
3. Pour 3 tablespoons olive oil and the lemon juice into a 9- by 13-inch microwavable glass baking dish and stir to blend. Place the fish in the mixture, turning the fillets over to coat on both sides. Arrange the fillets in a single layer. Tuck thin ends of the fillets under to ensure even thickness throughout.
4. Sprinkle the fish with 3 tablespoons parsley and thyme. Cover with the cooked onion and garlic. Arrange tomato slices on top and sprinkle the remaining parsley over the tomatoes.
5. Cover tightly and microwave on HIGH for 6 to 7 minutes, or until the fish flakes with a fork. Serve at once.

Serves 4–6

Raclette
Switzerland

The word raclette *comes from the French word* racler (rah-CLAY), *meaning "to scrape." Raclette is traditionally prepared by holding a chunk of the cheese before an open fire. When the cheese begins to melt, it is quickly scraped off with a large knife onto a hot plate. The cheese is then eaten with a boiled potato, gherkins (tiny pickles), and pickled onions. Swiss diners can easily consume two or three servings of* raclette. *Have extra ingredients on hand for big appetites!*

6 2-inch red or white potatoes, washed and scrubbed
¼ cup water
12 ounces (¾ pound) raclette cheese (or Gruyère or imported Swiss cheese)
12 small sweet gherkins
12 small pickled onions

1. Peel a strip around the middle of each potato. Place potatoes in a ring in a microwavable glass baking dish or casserole. Add water. Cover tightly and microwave on HIGH for 4 minutes. Rearrange and turn over the potatoes. Cover and microwave on HIGH for 4 to 8 minutes, or until tender when pierced with a fork. Let stand, covered, for 3 minutes.
2. Slice cheese into 12 equal pieces, each about ¼ inch thick and 4 inches long. Arrange 2 slices of cheese in the center of each of 6 microwavable plates. Microwave each plate, uncovered, on HIGH for 40 to 60 seconds, until the cheese is melted, creamy, and bubbly, but not runny.
3. Place a cooked potato, 2 gherkins, and 2 onions on the side of each plate. Serve immediately.

Makes 6 servings

French onion soup with cheese (right, recipe on page 27) or Swiss *raclette* (left) makes a delicious lunch or light supper.

Sweet cooked apples from Turkey (left) and baked bananas from Brazil (right, recipe on page 40) are sweet, warm endings to a perfect microwave meal.

DESSERTS

In many countries, no special celebration would be complete without the sweet pleasures of dessert. These desserts represent some national specialties—apples from Turkey, bananas from Brazil, sunny lemons from Italy, and heavenly Swiss chocolate. With the no-fuss, one-dish microwave method of preparing these desserts, you can easily add an international flair to any meal.

Sweet Cooked Apples/ *Elma Tatlisi* Turkey

Often stuffed with dried fruits such as raisins, dates, and nuts, cooked apples are a popular dessert in Turkey and throughout the Middle East.

4 medium Rome Beauty or McIntosh apples, washed and cored
16 whole cloves
½ cup sugar
3 tablespoons water
heavy cream or whipping cream (if desired)

1. Peel a 1-inch strip of skin around the middle of each apple. Firmly insert 4 cloves in the remaining skin around the top of each apple. Stand the apples in a round microwavable glass baking dish or casserole.
2. Spoon 2 tablespoons sugar into the center of each apple. Pour water into the dish.
3. Cover tightly and microwave on HIGH for 3 minutes. Turn each apple halfway around and stir the sugar syrup at the bottom of the dish. Cover and microwave on HIGH for 3 to 4 minutes. Let stand, covered, for 3 minutes. Serve the apples warm in their syrup, with heavy cream or whipped cream provided as an optional topping.

Serves 4

Baked Bananas/
Banana Bacana
Brazil

Desserts made of cooked bananas are popular all over the world. This version from Brazil, where bananas are a major crop, is a great dessert for lunch or dinner.

**3 tablespoons butter or margarine,
   cut into small pieces**
½ cup firmly packed brown sugar
1 tablespoon fresh lemon juice
2 medium bananas, firm and ripe
**2 cinnamon sticks, each broken in half
   rind of one lime, cut into thin strips**
⅓ cup sweetened grated coconut

1. In a shallow microwavable glass baking dish or pie plate, mix butter or margarine, brown sugar, and lemon juice. Microwave, uncovered, on HIGH for 1 minute. Stir well.
2. Peel bananas and cut them in half crosswise. Slice each half lengthwise. Arrange the 8 pieces in a single layer in the sugar mixture, turning them over once to coat. Put cinnamon sticks and lime peel around the banana pieces.
3. Microwave on HIGH, uncovered, for 2 minutes. Baste the bananas with the sauce. Microwave on HIGH for 1 or 2 more minutes, or until the bananas are soft. Let stand for 3 minutes.
4. Garnish with coconut and serve warm with the sauce.

Serves 4

Lemon Ice/
Granita di Limone
Italy

Granitas, or ices, are often enjoyed at outdoor cafés on warm afternoons in Italy. This slightly tart but refreshing dessert of frozen lemon syrup crystals is one of the most popular flavors.

2 cups water
½ cup sugar

**juice of 2 to 4 large lemons (¾ cup)
twists of lemon rind (for garnish)**

1. In a 1-quart microwavable glass measuring cup, combine water and sugar and stir. Microwave, uncovered, on HIGH for 3 minutes. Stir again. Microwave on HIGH for 3 to 5 minutes, until the sugar is completely dissolved and the water is simmering. Stir in lemon juice. Let cool for 15 minutes.
2. Pour the mixture into an ice cube tray (without dividers) or a shallow metal cake pan. Freeze for 1 hour. Then stir the sides and bottom of the pan with a fork to break up the ice that has formed. Repeat this process every half hour for 2 or more hours, until the *granita* has a firm but slightly slushy consistency.
3. To serve, scoop the *granita* into small dessert bowls or goblets and garnish with twists of lemon rind. If not serving right away, cover and keep frozen until ready to use.

Serves 6

You don't have to travel to Italy for the tart refreshment of *granita di limone*.

Chocolate fondue from Switzerland is a special treat for chocolate lovers. Choose your favorite fruits and sweets to dip in the rich, creamy chocolate.

Chocolate Fondue/
Fondue Chocolat
Switzerland

The word fondue *comes from the French word* fondre *(FOHN-druh), which means "to melt." This dessert, like the traditional Swiss* fondue *made with melted cheese, is easy to prepare and fun to eat.*

4 or 5 of the following (for dipping):
bananas, peeled
melon, peeled
pineapple, peeled and cored
grapes, washed
angel food cake
apples, washed
strawberries, washed and hulled
kiwi, peeled
marshmallows
6 ounces semisweet baker's chocolate, broken in small pieces (or semisweet chocolate morsels)
½ cup light cream
½ teaspoon vanilla extract

1. Cut the fruit and cake into bite-sized pieces and arrange on a serving plate.
2. Place chocolate, cream, and vanilla extract in a 1-quart microwavable casserole or handled bowl. Microwave, uncovered, on HIGH for 1 minute. Stir well with a wire whisk. Microwave on HIGH for 30 seconds or until the chocolate is thoroughly melted. Stir again until the chocolate is smooth and creamy.
3. To serve, place the dish of chocolate in the center of the table on a trivet or hot pad. Give each person a fondue fork or wooden skewer for piercing a piece of fruit or cake and swirling it in the chocolate.

Serves 6

THE CAREFUL COOK

Whenever you cook, there are certain safety rules you must always keep in mind. Even experienced cooks follow these rules when they are in the kitchen.

1. Read a recipe completely before beginning to cook. Make sure you understand the directions.
2. Always wash your hands before handling food.
3. Thoroughly wash all raw vegetables and fruits to remove dirt, chemicals, and insecticides.
4. Use a cutting board when cutting up vegetables and fruits. Don't cut them up in your hand! And be sure to cut in a direction *away* from you and your fingers.
5. Whether you use a conventional oven or a microwave oven, always use a pot holder to steady or handle pots and cooking dishes. Don't use a wet cloth on a hot pan or dish, because the steam it produces can burn you.
6. When cooking with a microwave oven, use cooking dishes that have handles or protruding edges that can be grasped easily with pot holders. Smooth-sided bowls of hot liquid or food can slip out of your hands when you carry them from oven to counter and cause accidents.
7. Lift the lid or plastic wrap from a microwave cooking dish by opening it away from you so that you will not get burned by the steam.
8. If you get burned, hold the burn under cold running water. Do not put grease or butter on it. Cold water helps to take the heat out, but grease or butter will only keep it in.
9. Operate the microwave oven only when the door is completely closed. Wait until the timer signals that the oven is off before opening the door.
10. Never use a damaged microwave oven or one that is not working properly.
11. If a fire starts inside the microwave oven, keep the door shut and turn the power off. Carefully disconnect the power cord. Have the oven serviced by a licensed repairer before attempting to use the oven again.

METRIC CONVERSION CHART

WHEN YOU KNOW		MULTIPLY BY	TO FIND	
MASS (weight)				
ounces	(oz)	28.0	grams	(g)
pounds	(lb)	0.45	kilograms	(kg)
VOLUME				
teaspoons	(tsp)	5.0	milliliters	(ml)
tablespoons	(Tbsp)	15.0	milliliters	
fluid ounces	(oz)	30.0	milliliters	
cup	(c)	0.24	liters	(l)
pint	(pt)	0.47	liters	
quart	(qt)	0.95	liters	
gallon	(gal)	3.8	liters	
TEMPERATURE				
Fahrenheit	(°F)	5/9 (after subtracting 32)	Celsius	(°C)

COMMON MEASURES AND THEIR EQUIVALENTS

3 teaspoons = 1 tablespoon

8 tablespoons = ½ cup

2 cups = 1 pint

2 pints = 1 quart

4 quarts = 1 gallon

16 ounces = 1 pound

INDEX

(recipes indicated by **boldface** type)

ABOUT THE AUTHOR

Nancy Cappelloni was born and raised in San Francisco, California. With degrees in art history and dance, she has worked as a parks and recreation director, a preschool teacher, a dance instructor, and a children's cooking teacher. Inspired by her students' enthusiasm for microwave cooking, Cappelloni gathered traditional recipes from around the world and adapted them for the microwave oven. She lives in Belvedere, California, with her husband and three daughters.

easy menu ethnic cookbooks